Valentine's Day
Día de San Valentín

Josie Keogh

Traducción al español:
Eduardo Alamán

PowerKiDS press™

New York

Published in 2013 by The Rosen Publishing Group, Inc.
29 East 21st Street, New York, NY 10010

First Edition

Editor: Amelie von Zumbusch
Book Design: Andrew Povolny   Traducción al español: Eduardo Alamán

Photo Credits: Cover, p. 9 KidStock/Blend Images/Getty Images; p. 5 Jupiter Images/Brand X Pictures/Thinkstock; pp. 7, 15, 21 iStockphoto/Thinkstock; p. 11 Digital Vision/Thinkstock; p. 13 Fuse/Getty Images; p. 17 LWA/Dann Tardif/Blend Images/Getty Images; p. 19 KidStock/Blend Images/Getty Images; p. 23 Fototeca Storica Nazionale/Photodisc/Getty Images.

Library of Congress Cataloging-in-Publication Data

Keogh, Josie.
Valentine's Day = Día de San Valentín / by Josie Keogh ; translated by Eduardo Alamán. — 1st ed.
    p. cm. — (Powerkids readers: happy holidays! / ¡felices fiestas!)
Includes index.
ISBN 978-1-4488-9970-8 (library binding)
1. Valentine's Day—Juvenile literature. I. Alamán, Eduardo. II. Title.
GT4925.K4613 2013
394.2618—dc23
                                                        2012022336

Websites: Due to the changing nature of Internet links, PowerKids Press has developed an online list of websites related to the subject of this book. This site is updated regularly. Please use this link to access the list: www.powerkidslinks.com/pkrhh/vday/

Manufactured in the United States of America

CPSIA Compliance Information: Batch #W13PK3: For Further Information contact Rosen Publishing, New York, New York at 1-800-237-9932

$16.95

Contents

Contenido

It is Valentine's Day!

¡Es el Día de San Valentín!

The day honors love.

_____

Este día celebra el amor
y la amistad.

Give a card.

_____

Puedes dar una tarjeta.

Teachers get the most cards.

Los maestros reciben muchas cartas.

11

Give a gift.

_____

Puedes dar un regalo.

12

Red **roses** stand for true love.

Las **rosas** de color rojo simbolizan amor verdadero.

15

Eat a treat.

Puedes comer un pastelillo.

17

Chocolate is the top-selling candy.

El **chocolate** es el dulce más vendido en San Valentín.

Lovebirds are from Africa.

Los **loros inseparables** son de África.

Cupid was the Roman love god.

_____

Cupido era el dios romano del amor.

WORDS TO KNOW / PALABRAS QUE DEBES SABER

chocolate

(el) chocolate

lovebirds

(los) loros
inseparables

roses

(las) rosas

INDEX

ÍNDICE

24